# Japanese Whiskey

With delicate notes of a young
woman's heart

Apoorva Nelli

BookLeaf
Publishing

India | USA | UK

Copyright © Apoorva Nelli
All Rights Reserved.

This book has been self-published with all reasonable efforts taken to make the material error-free by the author. No part of this book shall be used, reproduced in any manner whatsoever without written permission from the author, except in the case of brief quotations embodied in critical articles and reviews.

The Author of this book is solely responsible and liable for its content including but not limited to the views, representations, descriptions, statements, information, opinions, and references ["Content"]. The Content of this book shall not constitute or be construed or deemed to reflect the opinion or expression of the Publisher or Editor. Neither the Publisher nor Editor endorse or approve the Content of this book or guarantee the reliability, accuracy, or completeness of the Content published herein and do not make any representations or warranties of any kind, express or implied, including but not limited to the implied warranties of merchantability, fitness for a particular purpose.

The Publisher and Editor shall not be liable whatsoever...

Made with ❤ on the BookLeaf Publishing Platform
www.bookleafpub.in
www.bookleafpub.com

# Dedication

For Chrisphine


I miss you everyday

# Acknowledgement

My dear friend Ana, for always answering her phone through long distances and time changes, and always giving me solid advice about writing and life. My parents, although, at times found it difficult to accept me, never stopped loving me. For my friends through different walks in life who have chosen to love me for who I am, I am so very grateful for you. Lastly, to the love of my life, my dog Maximus, thank you for being there for me through some very tough times in life. Mama misses you everyday.

# Preface

This book of poems takes you through the journey of a resilient young woman as she courses through life experiencing confusion, love, abuse, loss, heartbreak, desolation, and difficulty finding her own identity. She keeps standing up after every hurdle and every blow life throws at her, and decides to choose happiness for herself. The hope is that the readers can relate to some of the poems and realize that they are not alone. Every person ebbs and flows through life which is why life is so beautiful. Remember, you are exactly where you are supposed to be, and you need to fight through the hard times to enjoy the fruit of the strength you gain through those experiences.

Happy reading!

I

Stuck in space
Emptiness
Weary faces
An illusion of exhaustion

Memories cramp
Mornings damp
Starless nights
An illusion of exhaustion

Coffee jitters
Grumbling stomachs
Bruising bodies
An illusion of exhaustion

Empty parks
Long dark walks
Masked smiles
An illusion of exhaustion

Hungry hearts
Loveless lives
Staring eyes

An illusion of exhaustion

**2**

I painted my nails black
I was fifteen
My hair was messy
My jeans torn
I wanted to hide
I wanted to be seen
All at the same time

I had opinions
Loud and strong
My audience were few
Mostly deaf and mute
What I said didn't matter
How I felt met with indifference

Another rebellious teenager, they said
"Can't you see" the words never left my lips
"I'm not angry, I'm hurting"
"I'm different, I know
But can you not accept me for who I am?"

I never could say those words
Instead, I brushed my hair back

And walked away
With my head held high
One day I will make a difference
I silently said to myself and smiled

3

He put his hand around my mouth
Don't scream, it's all fine he said
You're so beautiful, skin so brown
Hair so long, and smile so innocent
He licked my neck, grabbed my waist
Tried to touch me in my special place
"I just want to watch the sunset", I cried
My pleas didn't matter
Nor did the tears that rolled down my cheeks
I didn't want to miss the orange hues
I didn't want to set myself a curfew
So, every time I quietly crept on to the
terrace, I prayed
Please don't be there
And when he was, I silently said
"Let me go, I'm only eight"

# 4

Darkness falls
It always does
Behind the dreary air
Lies a light that shines bright
We never know what conjures it
A smile, a friend, a drink, or a notion
There lies hope even in distress
To keep you breathing
To keep you going
Because behind death, there's emptiness
Behind life, there lies a quest

5

When every good song you hear is blurred
There are words you want to say, but your
speech is slurred
All your thoughts are unclear and foggy
You want to see ahead, but the the horizons
are smoky
Close your eyes, my dear, and breathe deep
Your heart needs to lay still, you head needs
to sleep

6

You see my paintings
Filled with colors and shapes
Clear from the distance
Confusing within the space
"You're abstract" you say
"You can't be deciphered"
To each eye its own
Each heart is different

You fail to see me
What I am inside
I put on a show
But, I'm simple and mild
at heart. My head, now
that's a different story
I'm black and white,
translucent, filled with
glitter and gold
All at the same time

# 7

You always want the things farther away
"Oh so beautiful! Isn't God an artist", you say
The beauty takes your breath away
The thought of getting there fills you with
dare

You're so caught up in these far of thoughts
Of capturing the hidden and the mystic
You fail to see what you're surrounded by
Even though it's majestic

# 8

I was alone, not lonely
Nerding away happily
There was a void that I felt
Coming home to an empty house, I dealt
He pulled me in with an alpha's charm
Days became weeks, months passed by
I never questioned him nor asked why
I let him in, made him a part of me
I finally thought I had my fairy tale dream
We laughed, we travelled, had our bitter
sweet fights
It always felt right, seldom had dark nights

One day, I said I loved him, but I felt lost
He told me he cared, but couldn't bear the
cost
It was confusing, but I blamed myself
Later that week I found my fears
Secret love notes on his wall
He promised it was nothing, I was making it
all
I trusted him beyond my faith

He said he would set things straight
Things got worse, fights got long
I told myself, I should stop seeing monsters

I hated myself, I decided it was time but,
He held on to me tight, said "Baby, please
don't go"
How could I leave? I loved my man
So, instead I made love with all I can
I slept sound on his arm
In days I haven't felt that peace and calm
I woke up to see his cellphone chime
The devil in my head was back at his game
I hoped I was wrong, then found that text
Followed by his dirty, hurtful secrets
My heart shattered into pieces
Betrayal surrounded me like a cold blanket
I tried to close my ears to find some silence
Try I could but couldn't fix the pieces

9

I held on to you
Warm and close
Not because you made me feel safe anymore
But, because I'm a creature of habit

**IO**

It was just another day in February
I get a message from your friend asking if I
heard from you
We haven't spoken in three months, but I
never worried
Thought you needed your space

I told your friend, I haven't
To let me know when you call him back
I went about my day: work, gym, making
mundane dinner
Later in the night as I was retiring to bed
He called me, told me you were gone
Killled yourself
They found you lifeless, drowned in your own
stench
I didn't agree, refused to believe a word

I was hoping to wake up the next day
To hear it was all a joke
It wasn't
With every message and call, it became more
real

How can you be gone? You are my person
You never said goodbye, you never thought
about us
What were you going through that left you in
such an abysmal mess?
Whatever it was we could've figured it out
together
You for me, me for you, we always had each
other

It's two years later, a late night in 2021
I've thought about you everyday
When will your loss get any easier?
Will you show up one day and it won't be this
nightmare anymore
Or will I wake up one day and not feel you
around me no more

## II

With eyes of the purple skies
You see all the things that could've been
Lacking clarity in the deep blue sea
You get frustrated about the things that
could've been
Look at you, you beautiful resilient creature
You built yourself from ashes
But instead of celebrating your new born
wings
You keep thinking about the could've been
things

# 12

Glass that shattered
Plants that need to be watered
Curtains pulled close
Sheets that needed a fold

Milk that's gone sour
Bills need to be paid for power
The air has never been drier
There is no water

Through the slit in the curtain
Comes a ray of sunlight
It burns your half closed eyes at first
In the midst of darkness
Your eyes start to shine

Look at everything you created
You've grown from wanting to having
Yet, when it's quiet, you sink to the ground
Looking around at the empty room
Did you not work for this magic?
Then why does it fill you with gloom?

"When will I have it all?" You ask

# 13

I gave you me, to see you grow
From my blood and sweat
You found a grip to hold
My hand with yours

I pull you up with all my strength
You look into my eyes
"It doesn't hurt" I lie
"Hold on my darling" I cry

You stand on the ground
Excited to feel your feet
I lie down there, my hands are numb
But my heart is happy, because I found love

A love that wants to give without taking
And heal while breathing
I want to see you blossom
Without expecting your flowers

You say you want to run
Now that you can walk
You've never had that feeling

And now you can't stop

You want to see the world and smell the air
Of pretty girls breaking your heart
everywhere
I wish you luck and off you go
To far off lands on unknown roads

I sink to the ground
My knees are weak
My heart is heavy
I can barely breathe

"Go on, my darling" I murmur meekly

In the darkness of the night
You came to me to show your light
I did not want to believe you
Until I saw your shadow

I move with the cheer of a bird
What you don't know is I have no home
Trust in you I shall
After I see your shadow

The truth is I believed in light
The source and he who conjured it
Until it got dark and there was no spark left
And everything reduced to blurry silhouettes

Now I've learnt my lesson
There is beauty in darkness
For everything is laid in the open
To the heart that can see in the murky
shadows

# 15

Eyes of blue, brown and green
I've seen them all
They've pierced my skin and kissed my lips
Yet I feel more alive within closed canopies
And a tender touch

Abandoned and alone
I say I need my space
But never do I feel
More at home than when
I'm lost in the noise of the crowd

Why do I crave the acceptance
Of someone I barely know
Just because they give me
A tiny sense of belonging
Is it because my father could never
accept me for who I am
Or because my mother was too afraid
I'd have what she wanted for herself

Too frightened of being chased

I left fear of heights, loneliness and
materialistic things
Still I shiver in the quiet of the night
within the emptiness in my bed
Craving for your nails
To dig deep into my soft skin

# 16

One day this will make sense
To untie bonding without attachment
Tonight is not that time
To cleanse my mind
To comprehend the hurt and longing
How could it be?
Time was short
Yet, memories ran long
And feelings were profound
I trusted after what felt like eternity
Only to be shattered

There is no glory in loss
No ease in letting go
No meaning in holding on

# 17

How can I dream of being liberated
When I'm tied to the idea of you
How can I manage a life of growth
When I can only show you the bright side of
me

You see me laugh, charming everyone around
me
"Oh what a wonder she is" you think
She spreads joy everywhere she goes
She sparkles like a ray of sunlight
On the afternoon ocean

But when it's dark and the night is quiet
I lay awake under the covers
Thinking of all the pain I endured
and the strength it took me to move on
Fighting the fear of being pulled back into
the darkness

Will you like me the same
If you saw me coiled up in my thoughts?
Binding my wings with tape

So I can fit into a tiny box?
Will you see my charm before I burn down
Before I find myself again to rise up like the
phoenix

Will you?

# 18

Will you run through a closed door
Or will you try to find the key?
It is too dark to even see
If there is a switch somewhere
Your body tells you "Don't give up"

You struggle to get up on your own feet
Bruises? Broken bones? Signs of defeat?
Your will to escape is stronger
For there is a promise of love in the future

You've tried to dig into the earth
Now there's dirt and debris in your nails
All you feel is dry earth and scramble
Not a plant, no sign of life

You search around for water
Your throat is dry
Your thoughts start to squander
In despair, your fingers feel a touch of metal
A ray of hope, a hint of freedom

You crawl around in search

For a hole to fit, an answer to a new life
You desire to be blinded by bright lights
Walk and walk in circles you do
Who knows whether it's day or night

I am unwilling


 To accept defeat when it seems like there is
no hope
 To give up on myself because the end line is
near and I'm not close
 To pretend to know the answers and give up
a chance to learn
 To settle down for comfort when the road to
growth is unfamiliar

I am unwilling


 To accept that my destiny is set by anyone
except me
 That time dictates the life I want to create
and live
 That society sets the rulebook on who and I
how I love
 To stay in silence when people say things to
me that I can't comprehend

20

We tell ourselves we don't deserve happiness
all the time
That every good moment should be
interspersed with something sad
We look for a muse, a mysterious man that
needs unfolding
Someone who will make your heart ache, ends
his answers in questions

What if we have it all wrong?
What if we tell ourselves we deserve to laugh
all the time
To dance at stoplights and sing in public
What if we tell ourselves we deserve kindness
and love
And give it out to the world like we want to
take it in

Isn't happiness free?
Then why do we tell ourselves we need to
work for it
And why in the world
Should we wait for someone to give it to us

# 21

To be in the moment is the elixir of life
To let the body rest, the mind stay still
And thoughts run free
To dream, to smile, to breathe

This life is meant to be
One with the mountains, one with the seas
One as fresh as the spring flowers
As fierce as the thunderstorm winds
As peaceful as the sound of the ocean breeze
And as fulfilling as mama's hugs

This life is a tiny speckle in this big, beautiful
universe
The first ray of sunshine in the morning
The first drop of rainfall in the monsoon
The sound of a waterfall in the thick of the
jungle
The joy of summiting a mountain
All these form our within, and from within
Comes the joy to be

I give the universe myself,

my calm and my stillness
And in return I ask to stay free
As one of its innumerable creations
The way we are all meant to be